IMAGINATION
REMAINS OUR
MOST POWERFUL
ATTRIBUTE. WITH IT,
WE CAN ROAM
ANYWHERE IN
SPACE AND TIME

Will Artificial Intelligence Outsmart Us?

STEPHEN HAWKING was a brilliant theoretical physicist and is generally considered to have been one of the world's greatest thinkers. He held the position of Lucasian Professor of Mathematics at the University of Cambridge for thirty years and is the author of *A Brief History of Time,* which was an international bestseller. His other books for the general reader include *A Briefer History of Time*, the essay collection *Black Holes and Baby Universes*, *The Universe in a Nutshell*, *The Grand Design* and *Black Holes: The BBC Reith Lectures*. He died on 14 March 2018.

'Will artificial intelligence outsmart us?' and 'Is there other intelligent life in the universe?' are essays taken from Stephen Hawking's final book, *Brief Answers to the Big Questions* (John Murray, 2018).

STEPHEN HAWKING

Will Artificial Intelligence Outsmart Us?

JOHN MURRAY

First published in Great Britain in 2022 by John Murray (Publishers)
An Hachette UK company

7

Copyright © Spacetime Publications Limited 2018

'Will artificial intelligence outsmart us?' and 'Is there other intelligent
life in the universe?' are essays taken from *Brief Answers to the Big
Questions*, published by John Murray (2018)

A CIP catalogue record for this title
is available from the British Library

Paperback ISBN 978-1-529-39240-1
eBook ISBN 978-1-529-39241-8

Text design by Craig Burgess

Typeset in Sabon MT by
Palimpsest Book Production Ltd, Falkirk, Stirlingshire

Printed and bound in Great Britain by Clays Ltd, Elcograf S.p.A.

John Murray policy is to use papers that are natural, renewable and
recyclable products and made from wood grown in sustainable forests.
The logging and manufacturing processes are expected to conform
to the environmental regulations of the country of origin.

John Murray (Publishers)
Carmelite House
50 Victoria Embankment
London EC4Y 0DZ

www.johnmurraypress.co.uk

Contents

WILL ARTIFICIAL INTELLIGENCE OUTSMART US?

•

INTELLIGENCE is central to what it means to be human. Everything that civilisation has to offer is a product of human intelligence.

DNA passes the blueprints of life between generations. Ever more complex life forms input information from sensors such as eyes and ears and process the information in brains or other systems to figure out how to act and then act on the world, by outputting information to muscles, for example. At some point during our 13.8 billion years of cosmic history, something beautiful happened. This information processing got so intelligent that life forms became conscious. Our universe has now awoken, becoming aware of itself. I regard it a triumph that we, who are ourselves mere stardust, have come to such a detailed understanding of the universe in which we live.

I think there is no significant difference between how the brain of an earthworm works and how a computer computes. I also believe that evolution implies there can be no qualitative difference between the brain of an earthworm and that of a human. It therefore follows that computers can, in principle, emulate human intelligence, or even better it. It's clearly possible for a something to acquire higher intelligence than its ancestors: we evolved to be smarter than our ape-like ancestors, and Einstein was smarter than his parents.

If computers continue to obey Moore's Law, doubling their speed and memory capacity every eighteen months, the result is that computers are likely to overtake humans in intelligence at some point in the next hundred years. When an artificial intelligence (AI) becomes better than humans at AI design, so that it can recursively improve itself without human help, we may face an intelligence explosion that ultimately results in machines whose intelligence exceeds ours by more than ours exceeds that of snails. When that happens, we will need to ensure that the computers have goals aligned with ours. It's tempting to dismiss the notion of highly intelligent machines as mere science fiction, but this would be a mistake, and potentially our worst mistake ever.

For the last twenty years or so, AI has been focused on the problems surrounding the construction of intelligent agents, systems that perceive and act in a particular environment. In this context, intelligence is related to statistical and economic notions of rationality – that is, colloquially, the ability to make good decisions, plans or inferences. As a result of this recent work, there has been a large degree of integration and cross-fertilisation among AI, machine-learning, statistics, control theory, neuroscience and other fields. The establishment of shared theoretical frameworks, combined with the availability of data and processing power, has yielded remarkable successes in various component tasks, such as speech recognition, image classification, autonomous vehicles, machine translation, legged locomotion and question-answering systems.

As development in these areas and others moves from laboratory research to economically valuable technologies, a virtuous cycle evolves, whereby even small improvements in performance are worth large sums of money, prompting further and greater investments in research. There is now a broad consensus that AI research is progressing steadily and that its impact on society is likely to increase. The potential benefits are huge; we cannot predict what we might achieve when this intelligence is magnified by the tools AI may provide. The eradication of disease and poverty is possible. Because of the great potential of AI, it is important to research how to reap its benefits while avoiding potential pitfalls. Success in creating AI would be the biggest event in human history.

Unfortunately, it might also be the last, unless we learn how to avoid the risks. Used as a toolkit, AI can augment our existing intelligence to open up advances in every area of science and society. However, it will also bring dangers. While primitive forms of artificial intelligence developed so far have proved very useful, I fear the consequences of creating something that can match or surpass humans. The concern is that AI would take off on its own and redesign itself at an ever-increasing rate. Humans, who are limited by slow biological evolution, couldn't compete and would be superseded. And in the future AI could develop a will of its own, a will that is in conflict with ours. Others believe that humans can command the rate of technology for a decently long time, and that the potential of AI to solve many of the world's problems will be realised. Although I am well known as an optimist regarding the human race, I am not so sure.

In the near term, for example, world militaries are considering starting an arms race in autonomous weapon systems that can choose and eliminate their own targets. While the UN is debating a treaty banning such weapons, autonomous-weapons proponents usually forget to ask the most important question. What is the likely end-point of an arms race and is that desirable for the human race? Do we really want cheap AI weapons to become the Kalashnikovs of tomorrow, sold to criminals and terrorists on the black market? Given concerns about our ability to maintain long-term control of ever more advanced AI systems, should we arm them and turn over our defence to them? In 2010, computerised trading systems created the stock-market Flash Crash; what would a computer-triggered crash look like in the defence arena? The best time to stop the autonomous-weapons arms race is now.

In the medium term, AI may automate our jobs, to bring both great prosperity and equality. Looking further ahead, there are no fundamental limits to what can be achieved. There is no physical law precluding particles from being organised in ways that perform even more advanced computations than the arrangements of particles in human brains. An explosive transition is possible, although it may play out differently than in the movies. As mathematician Irving Good realised in 1965, machines with super-human intelligence could repeatedly improve their design even further, in what science-fiction writer Vernor Vinge called a technological singularity. One can imagine such technology outsmarting financial markets, out-inventing human researchers, out-manipulating human leaders and potentially subduing us with weapons we cannot even understand. Whereas the short-term impact of AI depends on who controls it, the long-term impact depends on whether it can be controlled at all.

In short, the advent of super-intelligent AI would be either the best or the worst thing ever to happen to humanity. The real risk with AI isn't malice but competence. A super-intelligent AI will be extremely good at accomplishing its goals, and if those goals aren't aligned with ours we're in trouble. You're probably not an evil ant-hater who steps on ants out of malice, but if you're in charge of a hydroelectric green-energy project and there's an anthill in the region to be flooded, too bad for the ants. Let's not place humanity in the position of those ants. We should plan ahead. If a superior alien civilisation sent us a text message saying, 'We'll arrive in a few decades,' would we just reply, 'OK, call us when you get here, we'll leave the lights on'? Probably not, but this is more or less what has happened with AI. Little serious research has been devoted to these issues outside a few small non-profit institutes.

Fortunately, this is now changing.

Technology pioneers Bill Gates, Steve Wozniak and Elon Musk have echoed my concerns, and a healthy culture of risk assessment and awareness of societal implications is beginning to take root in the AI community. In January 2015, I, along with Elon Musk and many AI experts, signed an open letter on artificial intelligence, calling for serious research into its impact on society. In the past, Elon Musk has warned that superhuman artificial intelligence is capable of providing incalculable benefits, but if deployed incautiously will have an adverse effect on the human race. He and I sit on the scientific advisory board for the Future of Life Institute, an organisation working to mitigate existential risks facing humanity, and which drafted the open letter. This called for concrete research on how we could prevent potential problems while also reaping the potential benefits AI offers us, and is designed to get AI researchers and developers to pay more attention to AI safety. In addition, for policymakers and the general public the letter was meant to be informative but not alarmist. We think it is very important that everybody knows that AI researchers are seriously thinking about these concerns and ethical issues. For example, AI has the potential to eradicate disease and poverty, but researchers must work to create AI that can be controlled.

In October 2016, I also opened a new centre in Cambridge, England, which will attempt to tackle some of the open-ended questions raised by the rapid pace of development in AI research. The

Leverhulme Centre for the Future of Intelligence is a multi-disciplinary institute, dedicated to researching the future of intelligence as crucial to the future of our civilisation and our species. We spend a great deal of time studying history, which, let's face it, is mostly the history of stupidity. So it's a welcome change that people are studying instead the future of intelligence. We are aware of the potential dangers, but perhaps with the tools of this new technological revolution we will even be able to undo some of the damage done to the natural world by industrialisation.

Recent developments in the advancement of AI include a call by the European Parliament for drafting a set of regulations to govern the creation of robots and AI. Somewhat surprisingly, this includes a form of electronic person-hood, to ensure the rights and responsibilities for the most capable and advanced AI. A European Parliament spokesman has commented that, as a growing number of areas in our daily lives are increasingly affected by robots, we need to ensure that robots are, and will remain, in the service of humans. A report presented to the Parliament declares that the world is on the cusp of a new industrial robot revolution. It examines whether or not providing legal rights for robots as electronic persons, on a par with the legal definition of corporate personhood, would be permissible. But it stresses that at all times researchers and designers should ensure all robotic design incorporates a kill switch.

This didn't help the scientists on board the spaceship with Hal, the malfunctioning robotic computer in Stanley Kubrick's *2001: A Space Odyssey*, but that was fiction. We deal with fact. Lorna Brazell, a consultant at the multinational law firm Osborne Clarke, says in the report that we don't give whales and gorillas personhood, so there is no need to jump at robotic personhood. But the wariness is there. The report acknowledges the possibility that within a few decades AI could surpass human intellectual capacity and challenge the human–robot relationship.

By 2025, there will be about thirty mega-cities, each with more than ten million inhabitants. With all those people clamouring for goods and services to be delivered whenever they want them, can technology help us keep pace with our craving for instant commerce? Robots will definitely speed up the online retail process. But to revolutionise shopping they need to be fast enough to allow same-day delivery on every order.

Opportunities for interacting with the world, without having to be physically present, are increasing rapidly. As you can imagine, I find that appealing, not least because city life for all of us is so busy. How many times have you wished you had a double who could share your workload? Creating realistic digital surrogates of ourselves is an ambitious dream but the latest technology suggests that it may not be as far-fetched an idea as it sounds.

When I was younger, the rise of technology pointed to a future where we would all enjoy more leisure time. But in fact the more we can do, the busier we become. Our cities are already full of machines that extend our capabilities, but what if we could be in two places at once? We're used to automated voices on phone systems and public announcements. Now inventor Daniel Kraft is investigating how we can replicate ourselves visually. The question is, how convincing can an avatar be?

Interactive tutors could prove useful for massive open online courses (MOOCs) and for entertainment. It could be really exciting – digital actors that would be forever young and able to perform otherwise impossible feats. Our future idols might not even be real.

How we connect with the digital world is key to the progress we'll make in the future. In the smartest cities, the smartest homes will be equipped with devices that are so intuitive they'll be almost effortless to interact with.

When the typewriter was invented, it liberated the way we interact with machines. Nearly 150 years later and touch screens have unlocked new ways to communicate with the digital world. Recent AI landmarks, such as self-driving cars, or a computer winning at the game of Go, are signs of what is to come. Enormous levels of investment are pouring into this technology, which already forms a major part of our lives. In the coming decades it will permeate every aspect of our society, intelligently supporting and advising us in many areas including healthcare, work, education and science. The achievements we have seen so far will surely pale against what the coming decades will bring, and we cannot predict what we might achieve when our own minds are amplified by AI.

Perhaps with the tools of this new technological revolution we can make human life better. For instance, researchers are developing AI that would help reverse paralysis in people with spinal-cord injuries. Using silicon chip implants and wireless electronic interfaces between the brain and the body, the technology would allow people to control their body movements with their thoughts.

I believe the future of communication is brain–computer interfaces. There are two ways: electrodes on the skull and implants. The first is like looking through frosted glass, the second is better but risks infection. If we can connect a human brain to the internet it will have all of Wikipedia as its resources.

The world has been changing even faster as people, devices and information are increasingly connected to each other. Computational power is growing and quantum computing is quickly being realised. This will revolutionise artificial intelligence with exponentially faster speeds. It will advance encryption. Quantum computers will change everything, even human biology. There is already one technique to edit DNA precisely, called CRISPR. The basis of this genome-editing technology is a bacterial defence system. It can accurately target and edit stretches of genetic code. The best intention of genetic manipulation is that modifying genes would allow scientists to treat genetic causes of disease by correcting gene mutations. There are, however, less noble possibilities for manipulating DNA. How far we can go with genetic engineering will become an increasingly urgent question. We can't see the possibilities of curing motor neurone diseases – like my ALS – without also glimpsing its dangers.

Intelligence is characterized as the ability to adapt to change. Human intelligence is the result of generations of natural selection, of those with the ability to adapt to changed circumstances. We must not fear change. We need to make it work to our advantage.

We all have a role to play in making sure that we, and the next generation, have not just the opportunity but the determination to engage fully with the study of science at an early level, so that we can go on to fulfil our potential and create a better world for the whole human race. We need to take learning beyond a theoretical discussion of how AI should be and to make sure we plan for how it can be. You all have the potential to push the boundaries of what is accepted, or expected, and to think big. We stand on the threshold of a brave new world. It is an exciting, if precarious, place to be, and you are the pioneers.

When we invented fire, we messed up repeatedly, then invented the fire extinguisher. With more powerful technologies such as nuclear weapons, synthetic biology and strong artificial intelligence, we should instead plan ahead and aim to get things right the first time, because it may be the only chance we will get. Our future is a race between the growing power of our technology and the wisdom with which we use it. Let's make sure that wisdom wins.

THE HUMAN MIND
CAN CONCEIVE OF
THE MAGNIFICENCE
OF THE HEAVENS
AND THE
INTRICACIES OF
THE BASIC
COMPONENTS OF
MATTER. YET FOR
EACH MIND TO
ACHIEVE ITS FULL
POTENTIAL, IT
NEEDS A SPARK

IS THERE OTHER INTELLIGENT LIFE IN THE UNIVERSE?

I would like to speculate a little on the development of life in the universe, and in particular on the development of intelligent life. I shall take this to include the human race, even though much of its behaviour throughout history has been pretty stupid and not calculated to aid the survival of the species. Two questions I shall discuss are 'What is the probability of life existing elsewhere in the universe?' and 'How may life develop in the future?'

It is a matter of common experience that things get more disordered and chaotic with time. This observation even has its own law, the so-called second law of thermodynamics. This law says that the total amount of disorder, or entropy, in the universe always increases with time. However, the law refers only to the total amount of disorder. The order in one body can increase provided that the amount of *dis*order in its surroundings increases by a greater amount.

This is what happens in a living being. We can define life as an ordered system that can keep itself going against the tendency to disorder and can reproduce itself. That is, it can make similar, but independent, ordered systems. To do these things, the system must convert energy in some ordered form – like food, sunlight or electric power – into disordered energy, in the form of heat. In this way, the system can satisfy the requirement that the total amount of disorder increases while, at the same time, increasing the order in itself and its offspring. This sounds like parents living in a house which gets messier and messier each time they have a new baby.

A living being like you or me usually has two elements: a set of instructions that tell the system how to keep going and how to reproduce itself, and a mechanism to carry out the instructions. In biology, these two parts are called genes and metabolism. But it is worth emphasising that there need be nothing biological about them. For example, a computer virus is a program that will make copies of itself in the memory of a computer, and will transfer itself to other computers. Thus it fits the definition of a living system that I have given. Like a biological virus, it is a rather degenerate form, because it contains only instructions or genes, and doesn't have any metabolism of its own. Instead, it reprograms the metabolism of the host computer, or cell. Some people have questioned whether viruses should count as life, because they are parasites, and cannot exist independently of their hosts. But then most forms of life, ourselves included, are parasites, in that they feed off and depend for their survival on other forms of life. I think computer viruses should count as life. Maybe it says something about human nature that the only form of life we have created so far is purely destructive. Talk about creating life in our own image. I shall return to electronic forms of life later on.

What we normally think of as 'life' is based on chains of carbon atoms, with a few other atoms such as nitrogen or phosphorus. One can speculate that one might have life with some other chemical basis, such as silicon, but carbon seems the most favourable case, because it has the richest chemistry. That carbon atoms should exist at all, with the properties that they have, requires a fine adjustment of physical constants, such as the QCD scale, the electric charge and even the dimension of space-time. If these constants had significantly different values, either the nucleus of the carbon atom would not be stable or the electrons would collapse in on the nucleus. At first sight, it seems remarkable that the universe is so finely tuned. Maybe this is evidence that the universe was specially designed to produce the human race. However, one has to be careful about such arguments, because of the Anthropic Principle, the idea that our theories about the universe must be compatible with our own existence. This is based on the self-evident truth that if the universe had not been suitable for life we wouldn't be asking why it is so finely adjusted. One can apply the Anthropic Principle in either its Strong or Weak versions. For the Strong Anthropic Principle, one supposes that there are many different universes, each with different values of the physical constants. In a small number, the values will allow the existence of objects like carbon atoms, which can act as the building blocks of living systems. Since we must live in one of these universes, we should not be surprised that the physical constants are finely tuned. If they weren't, we wouldn't be here. The

Strong form of the Anthropic Principle is thus not very satisfactory, because what operational meaning can one give to the existence of all those other universes? And if they are separate from our own universe, how can what happens in them affect our universe? Instead, I shall adopt what is known as the Weak Anthropic Principle. That is, I shall take the values of the physical constants as given. But I shall see what conclusions can be drawn from the fact that life exists on this planet at this stage in the history of the universe.

There was no carbon when the universe began in the Big Bang, about 13.8 billion years ago. It was so hot that all the matter would have been in the form of particles called protons and neutrons. There would initially have been equal numbers of protons and neutrons. However, as the universe expanded, it cooled. About a minute after the Big Bang, the temperature would have fallen to about a billion degrees, about a hundred times the temperature in the Sun. At this temperature, neutrons start to decay into more protons.

If this had been all that had happened, all the matter in the universe would have ended up as the simplest element, hydrogen, whose nucleus consists of a single proton. However, some of the neutrons collided with protons and stuck together to form the next simplest element, helium, whose nucleus consists of two protons and two neutrons. But no heavier elements, like carbon or oxygen, would have been formed in the early universe. It is difficult to imagine that one could build a living system out of just hydrogen and helium – and anyway the early universe was still far too hot for atoms to combine into molecules.

The universe continued to expand and cool. But some regions had slightly higher densities than others and the gravitational attraction of the extra matter in those regions slowed down their expansion, and eventually stopped it. Instead, they collapsed to form galaxies and stars, starting from about two billion years after the Big Bang. Some of the early stars would have been more massive than our Sun; they would have been hotter than the Sun and would have burned the original hydrogen and helium into heavier elements, such as carbon, oxygen and iron. This could have taken only a few hundred million years. After that, some of the stars exploded as supernovas and scattered the heavy elements back into space, to form the raw material for later generations of stars.

Other stars are too far away for us to be able to see directly if they have planets going round them. However, there are two techniques that have enabled us to discover planets around other stars. The first is to look at the star and see if the amount of light coming from it is constant. If a planet moves in front of the star, the light from the star will be slightly obscured. The star will dim a little bit. If this happens regularly, it is because a planet's orbit is taking it in front of the star repeatedly. A second method is to measure the position of the star accurately. If a planet is orbiting the star, it will induce a small wobble in the position of the star. This can be observed and again, if it is a regular wobble, then one deduces that it is due to a planet in orbit around the star. These methods were first applied about twenty years ago and by now a few thousand planets have been discovered orbiting distant stars. It is estimated that one star in five has an Earth-like planet orbiting it at a distance from the star to be compatible with life as we know it. Our own solar system was formed about four and a half billion years ago, or a little more than nine billion years after the Big Bang, from gas contaminated with the remains of earlier stars. The Earth was formed largely out of the heavier elements, including carbon and oxygen. Somehow, some of these atoms came to be arranged in the form of molecules of DNA. This has the famous double-helix form, discovered in the 1950s by Francis Crick and James Watson in a hut on the New Museum site in Cambridge. Linking the two chains in the helix are pairs of nucleic acids. There are four types of nucleic acids – adenine, cytosine, guanine and thymine. An adenine on one chain is always matched with a thymine on the other chain, and a guanine with a cytosine. Thus the sequence of nucleic acids on one chain defines a unique, complementary sequence on the other chain. The two chains can then separate and each acts as a template to build further chains. Thus DNA molecules can reproduce the genetic information, coded in their sequences of nucleic acids. Sections of the sequence can also be used to make proteins and other chemicals, which can carry out the instructions, coded in the sequence, and assemble the raw material for DNA to reproduce itself.

As I said earlier, we do not know how DNA molecules first appeared. As the chances against a DNA molecule arising by random fluctuations are very small, some people have suggested that life came to Earth from elsewhere – for instance, brought here on rocks breaking off from Mars while the planets were still unstable – and that there are seeds of life floating round in the galaxy. However, it seems unlikely that DNA could survive for long in the radiation in space.

If the appearance of life on a given planet was very unlikely, one might have expected it to take a long time. More precisely, one might have expected life to appear as late as possible while still allowing time for the subsequent evolution to intelligent beings, like us, before the Sun swells up and engulfs the Earth. The time window in which this could occur is the lifetime of the Sun – about ten billion years. In that time, an intelligent form of life could conceivably master space travel and be able to escape to another star. But if no escape is possible life on Earth would be doomed.

There is fossil evidence that there was some form of life on Earth about three and a half billion years ago. This may have been only 500 million years after the Earth became stable and cool enough for life to develop. But life could have taken seven billion years to develop in the universe and still have left time to evolve to beings like us, who could ask about the origin of life. If the probability of life developing on a given planet is very small, why did it happen on Earth in about one-fourteenth of the time available?

The early appearance of life on Earth suggests that there is a good chance of the spontaneous generation of life in suitable conditions. Maybe there was some simpler form of organisation which built up DNA. Once DNA appeared, it would have been so successful that it might have completely replaced the earlier forms. We don't know what these earlier forms would have been, but one possibility is RNA.

RNA is like DNA, but rather simpler, and without the double-helix structure. Short lengths of RNA could reproduce themselves like DNA, and might eventually build up to DNA. We cannot make nucleic acids in the laboratory from non-living material, let alone RNA. But given 500 million years, and oceans covering most of the Earth, there might be a reasonable probability of RNA being made by chance.

As DNA reproduced itself, there would have been random errors, many of which would have been harmful and would have died out. Some would have been neutral – they would not have affected the function of the gene. And a few errors would have been favourable to the survival of the species – these would have been chosen by Darwinian natural selection.

The process of biological evolution was very slow at first. It took about two and a half billion years before the earliest cells evolved into multi-cellular organisms. But it took less than another billion years for some of these to evolve into fish, and for some of the fish, in turn, to evolve into mammals. Then evolution seems to have speeded up even more. It took only about a hundred million years to develop from the early mammals to us. The reason is that the early mammals already contained their versions of the essential organs we have. All that was required to evolve from early mammals to humans was a bit of fine-tuning.

But with the human race evolution reached a critical stage, comparable in importance with the development of DNA. This was the development of language, and particularly written language. It meant that information could be passed on from generation to generation, other than genetically through DNA. There has been some detectable change in human DNA, brought about by biological evolution, in the 10,000 years of recorded history, but the amount of knowledge handed on from generation to generation has grown enormously. I have written books to tell you something of what I have learned about the universe in my long career as a scientist, and in doing so I am transferring knowledge from my brain to the page so you can read it.

The DNA in a human egg or sperm contains about three billion base pairs of nucleic acids. However, much of the information coded in this sequence seems to be redundant or is inactive. So the total amount of useful information in our genes is probably something like a hundred million bits. One bit of information is the answer to a yes/no question. By contrast, a paperback novel might contain two million bits of information. Therefore, a human is equivalent to about fifty *Harry Potter* books, and a major national library can contain about five million books – or about ten trillion bits. The amount of information handed down in books or via the internet is a 100,000 times as much as there is in DNA.

Even more important is the fact that the information in books can be changed, and updated, much more rapidly. It has taken us several million years to evolve from the apes. During that time, the useful information in our DNA has probably changed by only a few million bits, so the rate of biological evolution in humans is about a bit a year. By contrast, there are about 50,000 new books published in the English language each year, containing in the order of a hundred billion bits of information. Of course, the great majority of this information is garbage and no use to any form of life. But, even so, the rate at which useful information can be added is millions, if not billions, higher than with DNA.

This means that we have entered a new phase of evolution. At first, evolution proceeded by natural selection – from random mutations. This Darwinian phase lasted about three and a half billion years and produced us, beings who developed language to exchange information. But in the last 10,000 years or so we have been in what might be called an external transmission phase. In this, the *internal* record of information, handed down to succeeding generations in DNA, has changed somewhat. But the *external* record – in books and other long-lasting forms of storage – has grown enormously.

Some people would use the term 'evolution' only for the internally transmitted genetic material and would object to it being applied to information handed down externally. But I think that is too narrow a view. We are more than just our genes. We may be no stronger or inherently more intelligent than our caveman ancestors. But what distinguishes us from them is the knowledge that we have accumulated over the last 10,000 years, and particularly over the last 300. I think it is legitimate to take a broader view and include externally transmitted information, as well as DNA, in the evolution of the human race.

The timescale for evolution in the external transmission period is the timescale for accumulation of information. This used to be hundreds, or even thousands, of years. But now this timescale has shrunk to about fifty years or less. On the other hand, the brains with which we process this information have evolved only on the Darwinian timescale, of hundreds of thousands of years. This is beginning to cause problems. In the eighteenth century, there was said to be a man who had read every book written. But nowadays, if you read one book a day, it would take you many tens of thousands of years to read through the books in a national library. By which time, many more books would have been written.

This has meant that no one person can be the master of more than a small corner of human knowledge. People have to specialise, in narrower and narrower fields. This is likely to be a major limitation in the future. We certainly cannot continue, for long, with the exponential rate of growth of knowledge that we have had in the last 300 years. An even greater limitation and danger for future generations is that we still have the instincts, and in particular the aggressive impulses, that we had in caveman days. Aggression, in the form of subjugating or killing other men and taking their women and food, has had definite survival advantages up to the present time. But now it could destroy the entire human race and much of the rest of life on Earth. A nuclear war is still the most immediate danger, but there are others, such as the release of a genetically engineered virus. Or the greenhouse effect becoming unstable.

There is no time to wait for Darwinian evolution to make us more intelligent and better natured. But we are now entering a new phase of what might be called self-designed evolution, in which we will be able to change and improve our DNA. We have now mapped DNA, which means we have read 'the book of life', so we can start writing in corrections. At first, these changes will be confined to the repair of genetic defects – like cystic fibrosis and muscular dystrophy, which are controlled by single genes and so are fairly easy to identify and correct. Other qualities, such as intelligence, are probably controlled by a large number of genes, and it will be much more difficult to find them and work out the relations between them. Nevertheless, I am sure that during this century people will discover how to modify both intelligence and instincts like aggression.

Laws will probably be passed against genetic engineering with humans. But some people won't be able to resist the temptation to improve human character-istics, such as size of memory, resistance to disease and length of life. Once such superhumans appear, there are going to be major political problems with the unimproved humans, who won't be able to compete. Presumably, they will die out, or become unimportant. Instead, there will be a race of self-designing beings, who are improving themselves at an ever-increasing rate.

If the human race manages to rede-sign itself, to reduce or eliminate the risk of self-destruction, it will probably spread out and colonise other planets and stars. However, long-distance space travel will be difficult for chemically based life forms – like us – based on DNA. The natural lifetime for such beings is short compared with the travel time. According to the theory of relativity, nothing can travel faster than light, so a round trip to the nearest star would take at least eight years, and to the centre of the galaxy about 100,000 years. In science fiction, they overcome this difficulty by space warps, or travel through extra dimensions. But I don't think these will ever be possible, no matter how intelligent life becomes. In the theory of relativity, if one can travel faster than light, one can also travel back in time, and this would lead to problems with people going back and changing the past. One would also expect to have already seen large numbers of tourists from the future, curious to look at our quaint, old-fashioned ways.

It might be possible to use genetic engineering to make DNA-based life survive indefinitely, or at least for 100,000 years. But an easier way, which is almost within our capabilities already, would be to send machines. These could be designed to last long enough for inter-stellar travel. When they arrived at a new star, they could land on a suitable planet and mine material to produce more machines, which could be sent on to yet more stars. These machines would be a new form of life, based on mechanical and electronic components rather than macromolecules. They could eventually replace DNA-based life, just as DNA may have replaced an earlier form of life.

•

What are the chances that we will encounter some alien form of life as we explore the galaxy? If the argument about the timescale for the appearance of life on Earth is correct, there ought to be many other stars whose planets have life on them. Some of these stellar systems could have formed five billion years before the Earth – so why is the galaxy not crawling with self-designing mechanical or biological life forms? Why hasn't the Earth been visited and even colonised? By the way,

I discount suggestions that UFOs contain beings from outer space, as I think that any visits by aliens would be much more obvious – and probably also much more unpleasant.

So why haven't we been visited? Maybe the probability of life spontaneously appearing is so low that Earth is the only planet in the galaxy – or in the observable universe – on which it happened. Another possibility is that there was a reasonable probability of forming self-reproducing systems, like cells, but that most of these forms of life did not evolve intelligence. We are used to thinking of intelligent life as an inevitable consequence of evolution, but what if it isn't? The Anthropic Principle should warn us to be wary of such arguments. It is more likely that evolution is a random process, with intelligence as only one of a large number of possible outcomes.

It is not even clear that intelligence has any long-term survival value. Bacteria, and other single-celled organisms, may live on if all other life on Earth is wiped out by our actions. Perhaps intelligence was an unlikely development for life on Earth, from the chronology of evolution, as it took a very long time – two and a half billion years – to go from single cells to multi-cellular beings, which are a necessary precursor to intelligence. This is a good fraction of the total time available before the Sun blows up, so it would be consistent with the hypothesis that the probability for life to develop intelligence is low. In this case, we might expect to find many other life forms in the galaxy, but we are unlikely to find intelligent life.

Another way in which life could fail to develop to an intelligent stage would be if an asteroid or comet were to collide with the planet. In 1994, we observed the collision of a comet, Shoemaker-Levy, with Jupiter. It produced a series of enormous fireballs. It is thought the collision of a rather smaller body with the Earth, about sixty-six million years ago, was responsible for the extinction of the dinosaurs. A few small early mammals survived, but anything as large as a human would have almost certainly been wiped out. It is difficult to say how often such collisions occur, but a reasonable guess might be every twenty million years, on average. If this figure is correct, it would mean that intelligent life on

Earth has developed only because of the lucky chance that there have been no major collisions in the last sixty-six million years. Other planets in the galaxy, on which life has developed, may not have had a long enough collision-free period to evolve intelligent beings.

A third possibility is that there is a reasonable probability for life to form and to evolve to intelligent beings, but the system becomes unstable and the intelligent life destroys itself. This would be a very pessimistic conclusion and I very much hope it isn't true.

I prefer a fourth possibility: that there are other forms of intelligent life out there, but that we have been overlooked. In 2015 I was involved in the launch of the Breakthrough-listen initiative. Breakthrough-listen uses radio observations to search for intelligent extraterrestrial life, and has state-of-the-art facilities, generous funding and thousands of hours of dedicated radio telescope time. It is the largest ever scientific research programme aimed at finding evidence of civilizations beyond Earth. Breakthorugh Message an international competition to create messages that could be read by an advanced civilisation. But we need to be wary of answering back until we have developed a bit further. Meeting a more advanced civilisation, at our present stage, might be a bit like the original inhabitants of America meeting Columbus – and I don't think they thought they were better off for it.